Boatman, Pass By

poems by

Kathleen Holliday

Finishing Line Press
Georgetown, Kentucky

Boatman, Pass By

Copyright © 2023 by Kathleen Holliday
ISBN 979-8-88838-219-6 First Edition
All rights reserved under International and Pan-American Copyright Conventions. No part of this book may be reproduced in any manner whatsoever without written permission from the publisher, except in the case of brief quotations embodied in critical articles and reviews.

ACKNOWLEDGMENTS

Grateful acknowledgment to the editors and judges of the following publications and contests in which these poems first appeared or placed.

Cathexis Northwest Press: " Coven of One" "Early Astronauts" "Home Fires"
Fish Publishing Poetry Prize 2021: "Boatman, Pass By" (long-listed, judge, Billy Collins)
Ocotillo Review/Kallisto Gaia Press: "Going Feral"
New Ohio Review: "A Day at the Museum"
The Nimrod International Journal Literary Awards: The Pablo Neruda Prize for Poetry 2021: "In a Monastery Garden" (semi-finalist)
Poet Lore: "When Language Left Her"
The Write Launch: "The Gift of a Green Scarf" "The Last Days of the Dinosaurs" "Lifeboat in the Apocalypse" "The News of Your Death"

And to William Butler Yeats' poem, "Under Ben Bulben" for inspiring the title "Boatman, Pass By"

Note: La Serenissima—another name for Venice.

My heartfelt thanks to the Women Writers of the Salish Sea: Suzanne Berry, Brooks, Marty Clark, Iris Graville, Rita Larom, Ann Norman, Lorna Reese, and Gretchen Wing for their continued guidance, insight, and generosity. I am honored to be in the company of such literary citizens.

Publisher: Leah Huete de Maines
Editor: Christen Kincaid
Cover Art: Lofoten Islands, northern Norway. ©iStock.com/MAGNIFIER
Author Photo: Robert S. Harrison, www.rsharrison.com
Cover Design: Elizabeth Maines McCleavy

Order online: www.finishinglinepress.com
also available on amazon.com

Author inquiries and mail orders:
Finishing Line Press
PO Box 1626
Georgetown, Kentucky 40324
USA

Table of Contents

Boatman, Pass By 1

Early Astronauts 2

Home Fires 3

The Last Days of the Dinosaurs 4

In a Monastery Garden 5

Kitchen Ware 6

When Language Left Her 7

The News of Your Death 8

Coven of One 9

Voices at Night 10

A Public Display of Affection 11

The Gift of a Green Scarf 12

Rear-View Mirror 13

A Day at the Museum 14

A Life of Petrarch 15

Aloha 16

Going Feral 17

Thrive 18

Another Evening During Quarantine 19

Insomnia in Three Acts 20

Moderna Anxiety 22

Post-Moderna Anxiety 23

Lifeboat in the Apocalypse 24

*To my family
past
present
&
future*

&

*To the spirits
of this island
called home*

Boatman, Pass By

If that boatman were to float by
on this river of night
where I lie feigning both sleep
and death,

If he were to lean down
to check for coins to collect,
I'd open one eye and say,
I'm trying to sleep here.

Perhaps he's thinking of all
those other nights I hailed him
like a water taxi, when I prayed:
Anywhere but here,

How like me then, to be
early for an appointment
whether in Seattle or Samarra.

But there's one less thing
to worry about—it's too late now
for me to die young.

When it's time he'll circle back
for my body as freight,
my soul for currency.

And then, with his ear against
my cheek as if to ask,
Where to?

Like a tourist eager for a place
yet unseen, I'll say,
La Serenissima.

Early Astronauts

Those early astronauts
chimpanzees baring their teeth
gums exposed, careening in space,

were not, it was later learned,
expressing happiness,
but rather,

like us revolving around
the dark star of our father,
doing what he told us:
Smile for the camera.

Like our faces every time
we passed him by:
the rictus of fear.

Home Fires

We were born out of the same fire
a flicker of flame in our eyes:

my older sister—a raging pyre
her ululations, her song of self defense

my brother—a campfire, with firefighters,
cowboys like him, come in off the range

my younger sister—a bonfire to keen over,
cook over, where we warm ourselves

and me—a tiny ring of blue flame
I must tend, relight whenever it goes out.

The wind from the past smells of fire.
Some of us, still smoking.

The Last Days of the Dinosaurs

In third grade one afternoon,
we were ushered into the auditorium
for an animated film
about dinosaurs.

As comets and asteroids fell,
pocking the earth,
so did the huge creatures,
stumbling in their tracks,
long necks heavy.
When they hit the parched ground
the vibration shook the floor,
through my saddle-shoed feet
hooked over the bottom
rung of the metal chair.

When the last one lay down and died,
my throat closed, my eyes filled,
someone coughed, someone giggled,
a restless chittering in the dark.

The lights came on. We blinked
as black curtains swung open.
Outside, the sun glared down
over the playground.

Then we were let loose,
racing to swing on the monkey bars,
to hunt each other,
punch a tethered ball
around and around.

In a Monastery Garden

At the far end of the historical garden,
past the red barn,
the wheelbarrows overturned,
the lilacs long-since bloomed,
past the giant magnolia,
the monkey puzzle tree,

we reached up, my mother and I,
into the raspberry bushes,
so high we had to stretch,
thumbing the soft ruby caps into buckets.

A shimmer of light, a change in the air:
our arms now strong, our hands
creased and tanned with toil,
mine still the younger, the acolyte;
our sleeves, the coarse-woven gray of habits,
fallen back over our forearms.

And then she turned to me,
that smile I'd know anywhere,
her pail brimming.

Kitchen Ware

Those restless, furtive sounds I hear at night
from the kitchen—surely they're not

the toaster under its quilted cozy, murmuring
to itself like a bird in a cage

the coffee maker so content, so reliable

the stainless steel steamer, in high demand,
proud as a peacock fanning its tail 360 degrees

or the rice cooker squat, smiling like a happy buddha.

Perhaps the ones who don't get out much
have flung open the cupboards and kitchen drawers,
freeing themselves for a little excursion:

a gravy boat floats by, a runcible spoon for an oar.

a pair of bamboo salad tongs clack across each other—en garde!—

A can opener that once cranked around and around
can after can of cat food, idles without intent

and lying there, so treacherous, in a tray
among the blameless silverware: a corkscrew.

And now, a ladle, my mother's, that once dipped
and emptied out the darkness.

For so generous a measure, I have yet to find a use.

When Language Left Her

When the door between
the worlds stood ajar for her,

she told us, her children,
"I'm not coming back,"

as if we'd be tempted
to look for her in the eyes
of someone yet to be.

When language left her
just before she left,

the door opened wide
at a sign:

all the birds at the window
rose up, away, as one.

The News of Your Death

The news of your death
carried me like a runaway horse.

Pulling back on the reins
didn't help at all.

Grabbing handfuls of mane,
still I slid,
slid away,
thumping the adamant earth.

Message delivered,
the horse galloped free,
stirrups flapping,
back to the shadowed stall.

Clawing the grass for my glasses
I crawled, chest tight,
eyes wide with sudden knowing,

all breath bolted away.

Coven of One

She laughed when called
a water witch, and yet,

my mother,
a y-shaped stick in her hands,
divined water in the earth.

Rooted here
so far from the source:

Show me, mother, where to look,
show me again how it's done.

Now you're gone,
I thirst.

Voices at Night

On a winter night
Up North, I sat on my bed
reading a novel by Tolstoy,

the snarl of snowmobiles
cut through the subzero dark
like chainsaws.

I drew the curtain aside.

Headlights bounced over
whited fields, criss-crossing
over contours of several backyards,
trawling under clotheslines,
skirting the posts of buried
barbed wire fences.

When the noise finally
receded, I settled, found
my place in the book.

Out over the clear cold,
as if in answer,
a faint high lonesome
chorus of wolves.

I was sixteen then,
just beginning to understand
why voices sing
to the night,

why a woman would throw
herself into the path
of an oncoming train.

A Public Display of Affection

A ferry unloads at the Friday Harbor landing,
a parade of vehicles passes by, a rhythmic
thump, *thump,* thump, *thump*
as tires roll across the wooden dock.
Dogs hang their heads over half-open windows,
sniffing pungent low-tide,
other travelers stream by, hermetically sealed
behind tinted windows, air-conditioning.

Here comes a Harley in full-throated purr:
a woman riding pillion, black-leathered,
hair loose, helmet-free.
Two cigarettes between her lips,
she flicks a lighter and inhales,
taps the man in front, black-leathered too,
who reaches back for what she's lit,
who steers one-handed, grinning,
two plumes of smoke
trailing.

The Gift of a Green Scarf

Evening after winter evening
I knitted and purled a green wool scarf
for a boyfriend who, not knowing
it was intended for him,
remarked, "Awful color."

Night after night it grew,
spilling onto the floor,
longer than he was tall,

finally so long I wound it around
and around my own neck, over my ears,
my lips and nose.

That winter and every brutal blizzard
after, how that wool warmed me,

shielded my breath
from the icepack that formed
over my mouth,

how it matched my eyes,
that gift I made for myself.

Rear-View Mirror

Looking back, it was
the kind of romance that
makes me wonder now
if we should have exchanged
insurance information.

But no matter how far or fast
we went, the wind blowing back
my hair, neither of us owned a car,
let alone a license to drive.

Though truth be told,
I had a learner's permit.

A Day at the Museum

Despite blistered heels
in new shoes,
I can't seem to leave this gallery
of sarcophagi.

I limp closer to a glass case
where displayed *en pointe*
a pair of tiny sandals lies
pristine, and I wonder—
never worn?

Parting the stream of visitors
two statues rise monolithic
a man and woman, side by side
each an arm circling the other's waist.

Look at them, still standing
never turning back.

Look, I'd say, if you were here
how they've outlasted us.

A Life of Petrarch

The afternoon was hot.
Under the leafy shade
of elm trees in the park,

I looked up from
the biography of a poet
open across my lap.

There he stood, another one,
beside the stone bench
where I sat.

Though I don't recall
what day it was
or what I was wearing,

I haven't forgotten
subsequent evenings
and what he was not wearing.

Since then, I take note
of what interrupts
my reading,

how, often a book's a portent:
every woman he left me for
a Laura,

every life the sign
of an ending to come.

Aloha

The current man in my life
is the bobble-head hula dancer
who lives on my dashboard.

I drive fast
so his hips dip
his little grass skirt sways.

In his native tongue
a single word suffices
for two occasions.

Unlike the last one
how will I know
when he says goodbye?

Going Feral

With great humanity
my cats set a place for me

another bowl between theirs
where I assume
the bread loaf position
as we munch our kibble
companionably,
tails curled against our sides.

Later, they make room
for me on the couch
where we puddle together.

These acts of kindness—
as if they know how tough
it is being human these days
and what a mess we've made
of everything.

Thrive

We have become like newborns
in this uncertain time of isolation.

We may not thrive
deprived of the sustenance
of a full body hug, a handshake,
even the warmth conveyed
by a hand squeeze on the shoulder.

I thought I could breeze through
this—after all, as someone
of Scandinavian heritage,
maintaining a social distance
of six feet is no sweat,
(or, for my Canadian friends,
one hockey stick length).

But these long months
remind me I'm a cat person
whose cat companions are dead.
No warm being has leaned into my
embrace for some time now.

But I think too, how I've managed
all these years, though it hasn't been easy
living so close to the border
and never once touching Canada.

Another Evening During Quarantine

After dining alone,
I read late into the night,
so late, the owls in the trees
have ceased calling out,
"Who cooks for you?"
"Who cooks for you?"

Hours pass, the dark retreats.
My hands close the book,
held now like a prayer,
my ears attuned to the silence,
sure that when I hear it again,
I'll know the sound
of another heart beating.

Insomnia in Three Acts

I.
Those sheep I was counting on
huddle together in a shaggy vee,
head-first against the fence.

A black lab pads into the room
retrieving dead things
from the boneyard of my past.

Every time I say, *Drop it,*
he brings back another.

We play this game for hours
until he appears with bared teeth
smiling, and drops a yellow ball
into my hand.

Morning.

II.
I lie awake
trailing through dusty rooms
of a tiny house on wheels
for the answer to this
burning question:

What is the name of my
first grade music teacher?

Near dawn,
the answer bobs up
from a dark pool
like a Magic 8-Ball.

With a wave of her hand,
Mrs. Guard slows the metronome
of my heart
and finally, I sleep.

III.
Dying in a snowbank
is painless they say,
just like falling asleep.

But as a chronic insomniac,
I doubt it, I really do.

Which is probably why,
anticipating frostbite
before the numbness,

I find it hard to prise
my fingers from
this blanket of snow

and let myself surrender
to the oblivion of asleep.

Moderna Anxiety (COVID Vaccine #1)

I tell my reptilian brain
it's okay to stand down today.

My little arms waving,
bracing for a fight-or-flight
are too short to box with anyone.

I tell my reptilian brain:
let the body decide how best
to raise an army through
the long red marches of the blood.

I tell my reptilian brain
though asteroids fall,
glaciers recede, everywhere
ice is melting
again,

there is nothing today
these tiny arms can do but offer
one, and only then, will my reach
extend beyond them.

Post-Moderna Anxiety (COVID Vaccine #2)

I wake to darkness in a pool
of cooled sweat, limp from sleep

as if rigor mortis—routed for now—
lost a fevered battle for my body.

Free from pain, floating,
becalmed for hours, I lie

in the morning light entranced
by a song repeating itself.

Death must surely be that
place where no birds sing.

Lifeboat in the Apocalypse

I haven't always wanted to be
in the same boat with them

but when the time comes, I hope
there'll be room for me in that lifeboat
loaded deep with my siblings and other kin,

those who can do stuff:
my sisters who've fed multitudes
from their gardens, cooked every
family holiday dinner,
and my brother who's built homes,
fixed cars. I'll bet he can even start
a campfire without matches.

So today, when one of my sisters
snorted derisively,
What can you do in the apocalypse?

I said, I'll tell the tale around the fire
of how we survived,
like we did in that long ago story
of a mother and her children
adrift upon a raft.

I'll remember everything.
This time, I'll write it all down.

Born in the Pacific Northwest, **Kathleen Holliday** has lived most of her life there and in the Midwest. As a teenager, she emigrated with her family to Australia and then to Minnesota where she spent 22 winters before returning home to Washington State. Aside from poetry, she's writing about those experiences in two essays-in-progress: *Boomerang*, and *The Lefse of Two Evils*.

A graduate of Augsburg University and former library staffer with a passion for words, Kathleen's poems have appeared in many literary journals including *The Bellingham Review, Cathexis Northwest Press, New Ohio Review, Nimrod International Journal, Poetry Super Highway, SHARK REEF Literary Magazine,* and *The Write Launch*. Her first chapbook, *Putting My Ash on the Line*, was published by Finishing Line Press in 2020.

After decades of urban life, Kathleen is grateful to call an island in the San Juan Archipelago in Washington State—one of many unceded ancestral lands of the Coast Salish people—home.

www.ingramcontent.com/pod-product-compliance
Lightning Source LLC
Chambersburg PA
CBHW022128090426
42743CB00008B/1049